Printed in the United States
By Bookmasters

Continuing your Peanut Power journey

More Peanut Power

Avril Ann Lochhead

Illustrations by David Lochhead

BALBOA.
PRESS
A DIVISION OF HAY HOUSE

Balboa Press books may be ordered through booksellers or by contacting:

Balboa Press
A Division of Hay House
1663 Liberty Drive
Bloomington, IN 47403
www.balboapress.com.au
1 (877) 407-4847

Because of the dynamic nature of the Internet, any web addresses or links contained in this book may have changed since publication and may no longer be valid. The views expressed in this work are solely those of the author and do not necessarily reflect the views of the publisher, and the publisher hereby disclaims any responsibility for them.

The author of this book does not dispense medical advice or prescribe the use of any technique as a form of treatment for physical, emotional, or medical problems without the advice of a physician, either directly or indirectly. The intent of the author is only to offer information of a general nature to help you in your quest for emotional and spiritual well-being. In the event you use any of the information in this book for yourself, which is your constitutional right, the author and the publisher assume no responsibility for your actions.

Print information available on the last page.

ISBN: 978-1-5043-1085-7 (sc)
ISBN: 978-1-5043-1086-4 (e)

Balboa Press rev. date: 11/17/2017

Further food for thought

Peanut Power

and

Another Taste of Peanut Power

When very young, an elephant is tied to a short rope fastened to a stake in the ground.

This trains the elephant to stay within the limitations of the immediate area.

Even when fully grown, the elephant is not aware that freedom is there for the taking.

We, like the elephant have been conditioned.

Our habitual attitudes, thoughts and even feelings can immobilise us.

Our thoughts are the most powerful tools and fuel of creation.

We can use them negatively, or as suggested in this offering of peanuts, we can tap into our potential, unlimited greatness.

Add these peanuts your daily diet, and move in the direction of your dreams.

Allow them to enrich your experience of living, loving and your magnificence.

Have fun and play with these peanuts of thought.

Follow their trail to freedom!

$\mathcal{A}_{sk}$

for what you need to get what you want;
for support, for information, for help,
in order to clarify,
in order to discover what is possible.

Then be willing to listen for the guidance.
This is not being a victim.
This is the act of someone causing life
to go their way.

This page is for you to open your peanut

Your thoughts

Your feelings

Next steps

Beliefs

are there to be challenged.
Some still have value, keep them.
Other beliefs, when brought out into the light
of day can even seem absurd.
When they are not significant anymore they
are even laughable.

This page is for you to open your peanut

Your thoughts

Your feelings

Next steps

Courage

needs to have room to mess up.
To be out of control, out on the skinny branches
expressing yourself.
Learn, grow in everything you do especially
your mess ups.
This is where the juice lives – in the discovery
of the next steps.

This page is for you to open your peanut

Your thoughts

Your feelings

Next steps

$\mathcal{D}$iscipline

is the power of accomplishment in action.
Stay in training.
Do whatever it takes, even when you don't know.
That is when real creativity comes into play.

You have made it this far with your current answers
- what's next?

Great question!

This page is for you to open your peanut

Your thoughts

Your feelings

Next steps

*E*xpectations

can be truly life enhancing.
They can also get in the way, stop you saying
or doing what you need to say and do.
Expectations of yourself can habitually be used
to beat yourself up and invalidate yourself,
rather than to nurture and empower.

Expectations of others can surely beckon the
demise of intimacy.
Express your expectations responsibly.
Play with expectations, there is no "right" way,
only what works.

This page is for you to open your peanut

Your thoughts

Your feelings

Next steps

Forgiveness

or lack of it can be a source of suffering.
We are addicted to finding fault and blaming
someone / anyone.
Either, make suffering into an "art form"
- as some do. Or let it go!

Whatever happened - happened.
Now what?
Life ticks by, get on with it.
Set sail for your unimaginable future!

It's easier to blame, than be responsible for
having a brilliant and fulfilling life
- your choice!

This page is for you to open your peanut

Your thoughts

Your feelings

Next steps

Getting

specific about your
pathway and what
you will have happen -
now and in 2 years or 10.

How will your life look?
Feel?
Write it all down.
Travel?
Relationships?
Children?
Education?
Finances?
Is there a gap?

Work backwards, having accomplished your vision.
It will be easier to take the steps to its fulfilment.

What actions could you put in place now to
advance towards your dreams?

This really is a bit of a dance.
Sometimes a waltz, or maybe a tango even a
highland fling!

Enjoy the music!

This page is for you to open your peanut

Your thoughts

Your feelings

Next steps

Having

it all!

Well do you really want it all?

It will take a level of responsibility to handle it all.
Are you on for that?
In training for that?
Are you aware that you might already have it all; and have just been too busy to notice?

Look around and count your blessings.
Be present to having it all right now, and keep moving forward by contributing it all.

This page is for you to open your peanut

Your thoughts

Your feelings

Next steps

*I*ncluding

others; being appreciative of family, of children, of friends, colleagues, neighbours, Post Office attendants, Supermarket Cashiers.

Acknowledge they are all supporting you.

Appreciate other drivers thoughtfulness on the road, be civil to all, and watch your partnerships flourish.

This page is for you to open your peanut

Your thoughts

Your feelings

Next steps

*J*oke:

"This man dies and goes up to Heaven.
St. Peter says "Welcome. Great to see you!
- Now, did you have FUN?"

Think about it.

A Chinese proverb:
"Once man gets the joke he is
- he will never stop laughing!"

Laughing at yourself is super nurturing, and
highly health giving - you will last longer!

And enjoy a greater quality of life.

This page is for you to open your peanut

Your thoughts

Your feelings

Next steps

*K*nowledge

can be the biggest obstacle in the way of real progress.

What we already know - can stop us from discovering.

Use what you know as a springboard, an inquiry into what you don't know.

Maybe all an answer is useful for - is to take you to the next question.

This page is for you to open your peanut

Your thoughts

Your feelings

Next steps

*L*ove,

life and living - how to express ourselves in this minute is all we ever have.

Are you waiting, hoping, enduring or relishing, discovering new flavours ?

This is it - not a rehearsal!

We only ever have moments of NOW!

This page is for you to open your peanut

Your thoughts

Your feelings

Next steps

Miracles

are what happens when you get out of your own way.

Small Medium Large

Deserved Undeserved

Zero discrimination.

Maybe they are like buses - another one arriving soon.
Just signal you want it.

Have you received your miracle to-day?

This page is for you to open your peanut

Your thoughts

Your feelings

Next steps

Nests

are so important.
Environment is everything.
Physical, emotional, financial.
Internal and external.
Keep them all in order.

Clear them out regularly, old clothes, old habits
old thoughts can all clutter your progress.

Take care of your nests, make sure there is space
for new life to appear and flourish.

This page is for you to open your peanut

Your thoughts

Your feelings

Next steps

*O*utrageous

Self-expression.

Practice, fake it - till you make it!

Find a couple of friends, or if you have children include them.
Learn from your children, ask them to coach you as sometimes we have forgotten how to play full-out.

Outrageously self-expressed this lifetime!

How will you be outrageously Self-expressed today?

This page is for you to open your peanut

Your thoughts

Your feelings

Next steps

*P*ermission

is necessary before anything else can happen.

Giving yourself permission to let go of the past, to move forward, to trust yourself and others, believe and create another future.

To be unstoppable.
Include other opinions and when necessary, decline them.

You need to be fully in the driver's seat of your life.

This page is for you to open your peanut

Your thoughts

Your feelings

Next steps

Questions

are vital for growth and development.

And it may not be your answers that make the difference.

Answers are useful momentarily, although they can often provide more of the same.

Growth and development is another phenomenon.

It will require asking questions that you have never asked before. Now there's a challenge!

This page is for you to open your peanut

Your thoughts

Your feelings

Next steps

*R*espect

yourself, have compassion for where you are, and where you are not - yet.

When you congratulate yourself on each step in your progress, you are free to really enjoy the journey.

Bring respect to your relationship with others, especially children, they are our future, honour and appreciate their contribution.

This page is for you to open your peanut

Your thoughts

Your feelings

Next steps

Standards

are always being challenged.

"Children should be seen and not heard!"

"Don't talk back to your elders!"

How can children ever make a difference?
Or how can we contribute to people more senior
in years than ourselves?

When challenging inherited standards, we
can see they could be very limiting and even
confine you to playing a "role".

Life is too short, do not let the future be limited
by the past!

This page is for you to open your peanut

Your thoughts

Your feelings

Next steps

$\mathcal{T}$rusting

yourself is paramount to growth.
The buck and everything else stops here.

Now this may not be good news.
Or, you are already in the process of mastering
your destiny.

Either way, you are "the one" in your life.

Make sure your voice matters, make a positive
difference in the areas of life that are important
to you.

Go for it!!

This page is for you to open your peanut

Your thoughts

Your feelings

Next steps

*U*pset

can be a familiar, knee-jerk reaction.
A sense of "flight or fight or freeze".

You may have been distracted by a old and
likely habitual way of being, thinking or acting.

There will always be an instant to...
Stop Listen Re-Think Choose

Then be, think and act in an alternative,
nurturing and responsive way.

Practicing these new skills to break the
automatic and often negative patterns can
create new futures.

This page is for you to open your peanut

Your thoughts

Your feelings

Next steps

Victories

in life are worth celebrating.

Listen out for them, feel them.
Appreciate yourself for noticing them.

Every moment to-day could be an embryonic
victory.
Anticipate them....

Be victorious, then watch life line up with you.

This page is for you to open your peanut

Your thoughts

Your feelings

Next steps

Wonder

is regaining a childlike and playful appreciation of life's journey.

It removes the significance and it is replaced by curiosity, risking and savouring the discoveries made along the way.

Nothing is ever wrong, when you are full of wonder of what can be next?

This page is for you to open your peanut

Your thoughts

Your feelings

Next steps

*X*pensive

lessons are the ones from which we do not learn.

There is a cost to growth, and only you can determine if you are getting life enhancing value.

Are you appreciating how far you have come?

Take a few moments to stop and acknowledge all those life giving steps already taken.

This page is for you to open your peanut

Your thoughts

Your feelings

Next steps

$\mathcal{Y}$outh

is often thought of as being rebellious.

Don't let your "age" distract you.

Be youthful now - even rebellious!

Positive change at any time can be accomplished little by little.

Become a revolutionary on behalf of "what works".

Take care of yourself, then take care of others.

This page is for you to open your peanut

Your thoughts

Your feelings

Next steps

Zany

is good, we could all use a bit more joy, celebration and fun.

Nurture the child within, be childlike
- as opposed to childish.

Honour and take care of your small person, appreciate them daily - with lots of hugs.

And move powerfully in the world as an adult.

This page is for you to open your peanut

Your thoughts

Your feelings

Next steps

About the author

Avril Ann Lochhead is an enthusiastic and visionary trainer, whose results in personal empowerment are an unqualified success.

As a transitional specialist, Avril believes we can go beyond our previous thinking to access new levels of fulfillment we desire for ourselves, our families and our communities.

Embracing current circumstances, trusting an internal feeling of respect and esteem for your "Self", are the fundamental ingredients of being fulfilled.

When this relationship with yourself is regained and fully expressed, you can then expand - and offer your contribution, generosity and appreciation to others.

Your life takes on a truly magnificent flavour.

May all your peanuts be positive!